Ur

Together We Can

Mc
Graw
Hill
Education

Contents

Rooster and Goose

Life at the farm was like a wild zoo!
Rooster and Goose felt that they
should come up with a plan. Things
needed to run smoother.

1

First, Rooster and Goose brought the animals through the big barn door. Rooster said, "We know you are busy, but we need to make the farm better. We have an answer to fix it up!"

Then Goose stated, "Let's not bug each other. Let's join together! We can make it better!"

So, Rooster and Horse went to check the crops. They set the roots in and scooped soil on top. This was enough to make the crops grow.

The chicks picked up the hay. Then, Goose and Pig made the hay neat. The eyes of the animals were wide with joy. The farm looked so nice!

That night, the animals sat under the bright moon. They were glad that they came together and did the job. The farm felt like such a nicer place.

Rooster and Goose both said, "It is cool to be a team!"

Choose a Room

If we looked around this house, we may see a mess in some rooms. If we brought the right tools, we might join in together and end the mess.

Hero/age fotostock

First, we can clean the kitchen. Put away the clean forks and spoons. Use a broom to sweep. This room will keep us busy!

Then, we can go to a bedroom. Scoop up any loose clothes. Make the bed. If it looks clean enough to all eyes, we move on.

Now, go to the other rooms. Don't be too noisy or it will sound like a zoo! We clean until the rooms shine.

Around noon, we can go outside to clean. We can rake and pick up trash, too. Don't clean the pool or roof. That's not safe for us!

You might find that you enjoy cleaning up a house. If we work together, it can go very well. Then, we can take a rest. The cleaning team can sit down in the shade and have a cool drink!

The Flute Youth

June and Jude are good pals.
They like to listen to lots of tunes.
They like the sound of loud drums
and the noise of a big sax.

9

One day, June said, "Let's start a flute group! We can play in a band and make up fun tunes."

With wide eyes, Jude said, "Oh boy, that sounds like fun! We can go to each door and ask our pals. I hope we get enough answers to start our band."

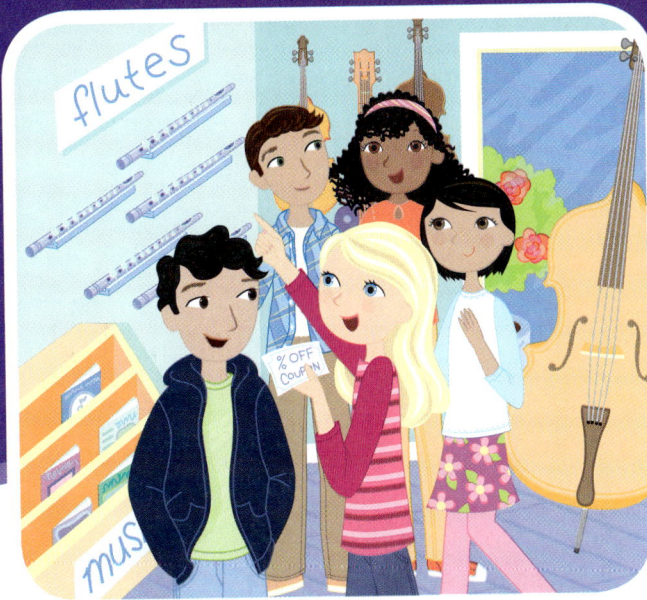

Jude and June found many pals
to join them. Then, they went to a
busy store that had things for the
band.

"We need to buy the right stuff.
I brought a coupon that we can
use. We can get five flutes!"
said June.

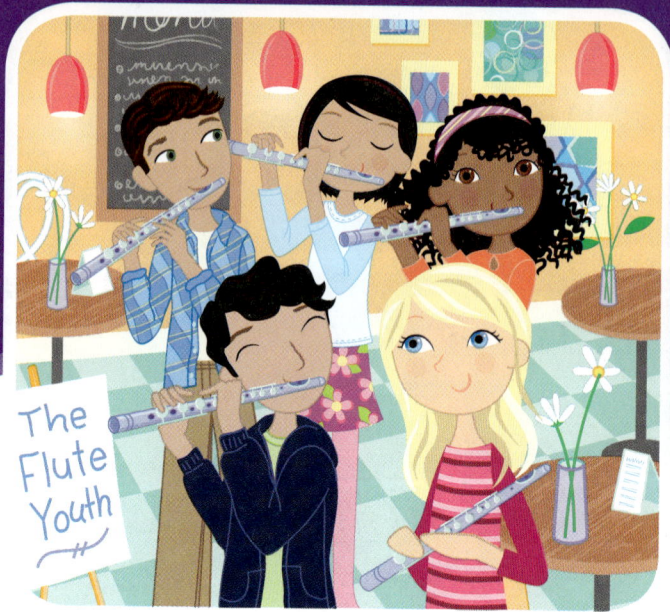

The band needed one last thing. "What should our name be? The Flute Dudes? The Cougars?" asked Jude.

June said, "I like those names you have, but I think we need a name that fits us best. We should be called The Flute Youth!"

Group Rules

It takes a good group to get a big job done. When you work together, group rules help. Rules make sure that a job is done in the right way.

Sue Green/iStockphoto/Getty Images

If it is winter, a group might need to get rid of snow. You can make a rule to take turns. That will keep the group busy. When it gets cold, Mom or Dad can serve hot soup that they brought for the group! That is a treat the group can enjoy!

If it is summer, it might be hot enough for a group to go to the beach! If you make a house in the sand, make rules. No sand can fly, and pals take turns! One pal can make the door. Another pal can make a window.

These rules are good all the time. One rule is to not be rude or mean. Another rule is to not annoy the group. These rules should not hurt a pal's feelings.

Group rules can help youth or older people work together. So use them!

Lewis and His New Suit

Lewis was a boy who liked to work alone. He thought he had the right answers. Lewis did not want help from any pals.

One day, Lewis had his new suit with him. He sat to drink a can of fruit juice. A big wind blew it from his hand and it got on his suit. What a mess!

Lewis closed his eyes and wished for the suit to get clean. It did not work. Lewis felt sad enough to cry.

18

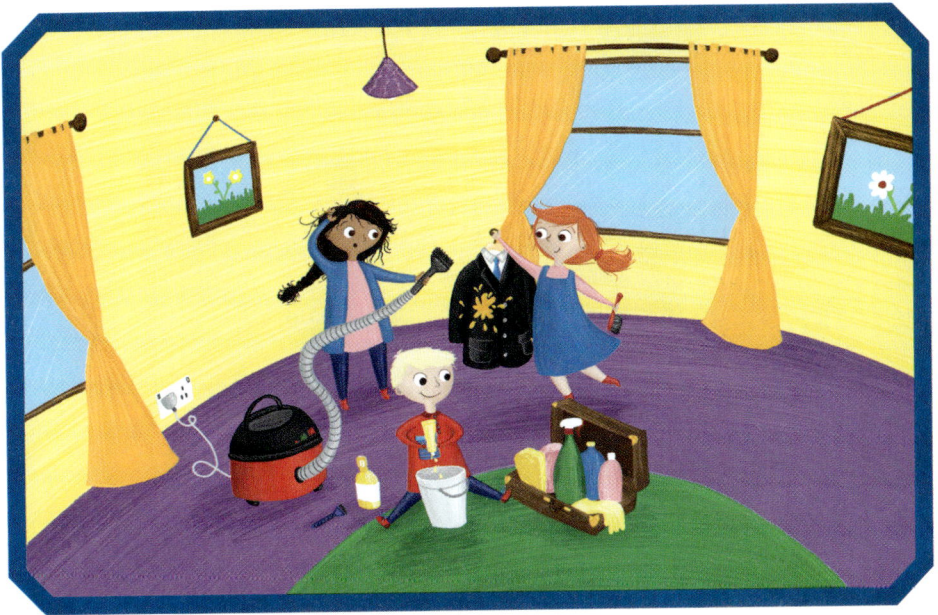

Lewis went home. He did not have a good plan. Just then, there was a noise at his door. When Lewis opened it, a crew came in!

The crew brought a suitcase filled with things to clean the suit. Soon, the fruity stain was clean! Lewis had a big grin on his face.

Now, Lewis helps the crew, and the crew helps Lewis. They drew up a plan to make things work.

Lewis helps the crew, even if he is very busy. The crew makes the time for Lewis. It's a good plan!

A Cruise Crew

Have you been on a cruise? A cruise is a trip on a ship. On a cruise, a busy team must work together to make it a fun and safe trip.

21

Some people on a cruise help with the food. This crew makes sure there is enough fresh fruit and juice brought out. You may want a yummy treat to chew. The crew can get it for you!

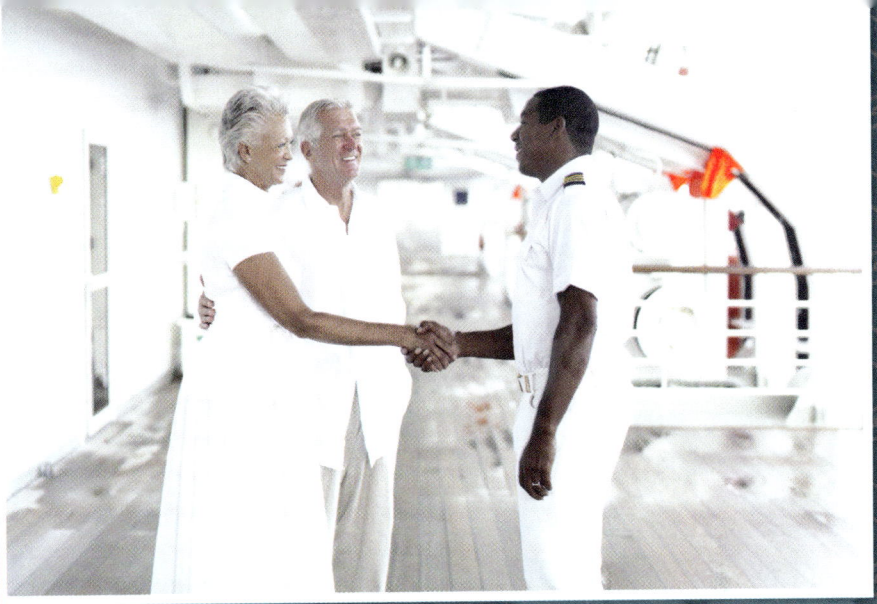

LWA/Photodisc/Getty Images

If you get a bruise, the crew will help. If you call because the key to a door is lost, the crew will answer. If the wind blew a new toy away, the crew will get it!

Some of the crew are in suits. The crew in white suits help with the big jobs on the ship.

23

The crew of a cruise ship is a good team. They can help all the people on the big ship. The crew takes pride in the role they play.

So join a crew on the sea. You will have a fun time!

Sue and Lucy

Sue and Lucy were pals. They were students in the same class. Sue's home was right next door to Lucy's. Sue and Lucy did it all together.

One day, Lucy had the flu. She felt quite bad and had to sleep. When Sue came over, Lucy did not answer. Sue felt sad and blue. Then, Lucy's mom came to the door. She said, "I wish this was not true, but Lucy is sick. Can you get her work from school?"

Sue was busy at school, but she got work for Lucy. She brought glue and paper, so that Lucy could do her art. Sue gave them to Lucy's mom. Lucy used the glue and paper to make a bluebird. She made it by joining the bits of paper to make a bird.

When Lucy felt well enough, she showed her art to Sue. Sue's eyes were wide! She said, "You must feel so much better. That art is super! And that's the truth!"

"You are a true pal, Sue," said Lucy as she hugged Sue with joy.

A True Team

In a class, students might join a team. Each student in the team must do enough to help. Each student must tell the truth, too.

If a team has to find an answer, the team should keep an eye out for clues. An answer might be about a bluebird or Pluto.

The team can look for the right answers in many ways. Students can get busy by looking in a book or by using a laptop.

Chris Bernard/E+/Getty Images

If a team has to make art, one student can get glue. Another might take out red paint. Then, the team can make a true work of art!

If it is super, the team may want to hang it on a door.

It would be cruel for a team of students to not work together. A team must get the job done and not be untrue to each other. A team should have a good plan. They must use the right things. Then, they can enjoy a job well done!

Paul's Paw

Lou had a dog named Paul. When Paul plays, he can hurt himself. Once, he hurt his jaw because he chewed a hard toy. Today, Paul hurt his paw.

Lou had to call his mother, father, and brother to come and help. Then, Dad put Paul in his car and hauled him to the vet.

The vet saw Paul's paw and said, "I think Paul's paw will be fine, but he may have to crawl a bit."

Lou felt awful. He had to pause so that he would not bawl. Lou said, "Paul is my best friend! I love him. It is my fault that he got hurt."

The vet said, "No, Lou. Paul is a super dog, but dogs get hurt. At least he does not have the flu!"

They took Paul home to get some rest. Lou drew a picture of the vet in a blue suit. Lou said, "I think that vet is a cool gal!"

"Woof!" barked Paul with a grin.

Lou could tell that Paul was on the mend. Lou hugged his big dog friend.

Thank You Authors!

If you love to read, then you can thank an author. Authors help us to pause and make a picture in our minds when we read books.

37

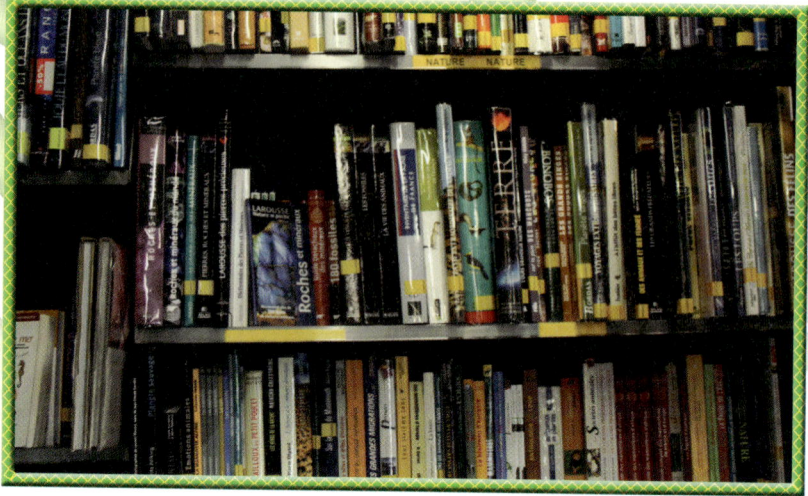

When you choose a book, think about the words inside. Is the book about a hawk? Is the book about men who will launch a rocket?

An author uses all kinds of words. An author can cause you to think about a lot of things.

Erica Simone Leeds

Image Source/Photodisc/Getty Images

We can all find good books. Brothers and sisters can read about haunted houses. Mothers and fathers can read about lawns, bikes, or autos.

Some authors can draw, too! They might draw a new land or a shark with big teeth.

At dawn, you can wake up, yawn, and grab a book. You can call a friend and read together. What do you like to read?

If you met an author, what words would you use? What would you say to him or her? You can say, "Thank you!"

Not Too Small

Judy's mother and father took her and her pals to the park every day. A group of big bugs always played ball. They played from morning to night. They loved to play, but not with the small bugs.

"Can we play ball with you?"
Judy asked. "My friend and I
might be smaller than you, but
we want to play. My brother
also wants to play!"

"You are too small to play with
us!" answered the big bugs.

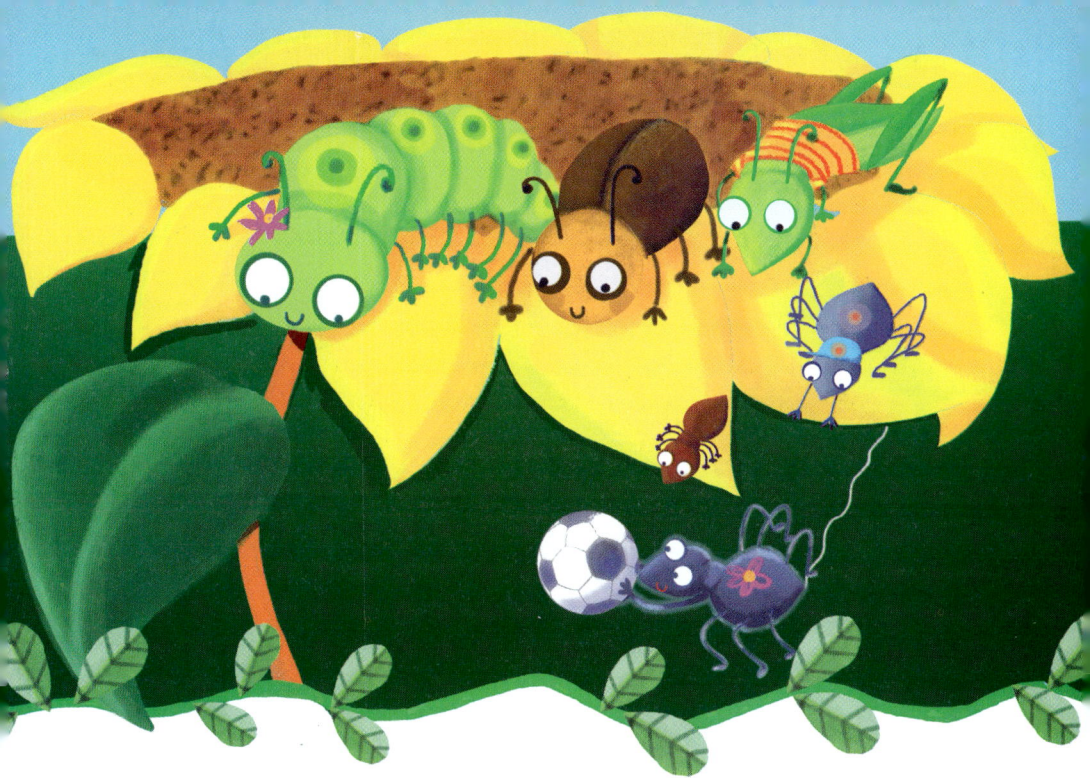

Just then, the wind blew. The ball started to fall over the edge! Judy was very fast. She spun a web. She caught the ball just in time. "You saved the ball!" said the big bugs. All of the bugs thanked Judy.

Then the big bugs taught the small bugs how to play. All the bugs played together. Judy caught the ball. One bug took a picture. It was a fun time!

A big bug said, "You can help us just like we can help you. It is good to be small!"

My Baseball Coach

My baseball coach is a big help. He shows me new things all the time. He also teaches me to not be rude or naughty. He is a super coach!

When I caught my first ball, my coach was so proud. He even called my mother and father to tell them about the catch.

His daughters play on our team, too. One daughter can hit the ball hard. The other caught a pop up ball to win our last game.

Ryan McVay/Photodisc/Getty Images

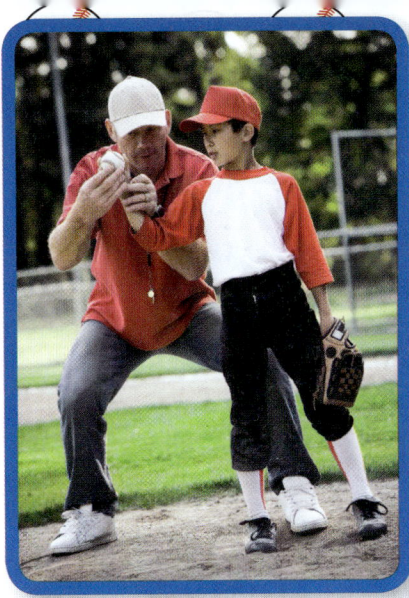

My coach taught me how to pitch. I can pitch fast or slow. My best friend comes to try and hit my pitches. I love to pitch! When I pitch, I just try to picture a small spot. Then, I aim the ball at that spot. I don't always hit that spot. Oh, well! I can just try more pitches another day.

Anderson Ross/Photodisc/Getty Images

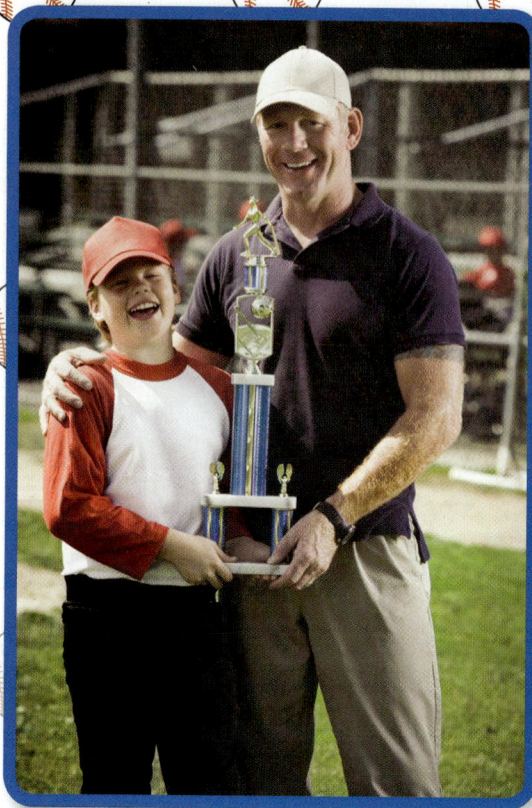

Anderson Ross/Flickr Open/Getty Images

If I fall and get a bruise or a cut in a game, my coach will help me feel better. He helps me play the best ball I can. I love baseball!

A Walk with Mayor Moose

Moose is the new mayor of the town. Each animal had a vote, and they chose Moose. Moose's job is to walk and talk to each animal.

49

On Monday, Moose walked to see Raven. He had the flu and felt bad. Moose talked with him to see if she could help Raven.

Raven said, "Thank you! You are a good mayor and friend. But my mother and father can help. I will fly again real soon!"

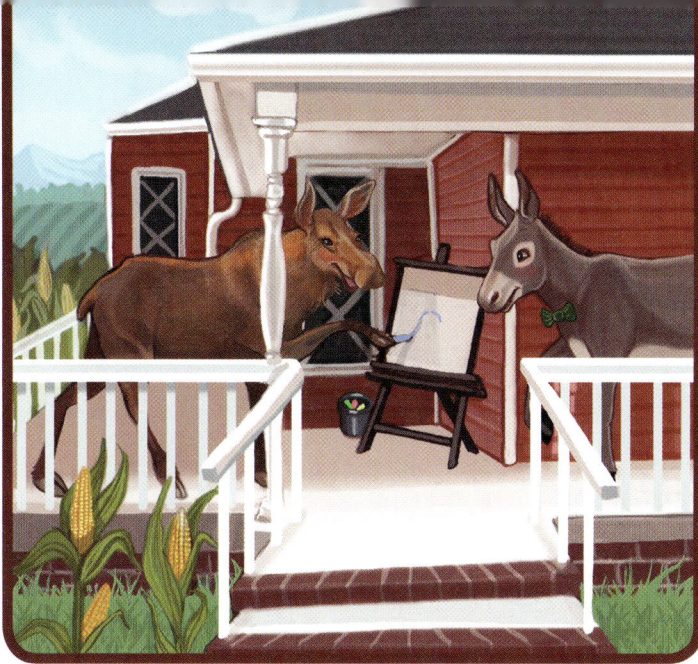

Then, Moose went to see Mule. Moose walked through high corn stalks to find Mule's house.

Mule had paper and chalk in a can. Mule said, "It is nice to see you. I do need help. My brother loves art, so can you help make a picture for him with this blue chalk?"

Art did not suit Moose, but she still drew that picture! Mule showed all his friends. Moose will help any animal who asks!

Moose walks around town each day. She talks to all animals she meets. The town loves her. Moose is the town's best mayor yet!

Teacher Talk

LWA/Dann Tardif/Blend Images/Corbis

A teacher can help. When you do a task, a teacher can talk with you to make it less hard. A teacher is like a mother or father at school!

A teacher might use chalk or a marker to put work on the board. The chalk might be white or blue. A student can walk to the board and do the work. If the student is not right, the teacher talks with him or her about a new way to answer it.

Some teachers can help with art. You may want to draw a corn stalk. A teacher can walk over to show you how to draw it.

Teachers also help with math and reading. They will teach you to read a book. They will teach you to add and find the sum.

Christopher Futcher/Vetta/Getty Images

Yes, teachers can help you.
A brother or sister would love to help you, too. A friend can also lend a hand.

If teachers have walked up and talked with you, then you know how much you learned from these great people.

Miss Wright's Job

Miss Wright came to class to show students a map. The children had seen her on the news. She was there to talk about her job.

Miss Wright pointed to a large map on the wall. It showed clouds, sun, wind, snow and rain.

Then, Miss Wright said, "I've been on TV for six years. I predict when storms are headed our way. I read maps and reports, but sometimes I am wrong.

Miss Wright showed a picture of a big spinning cloud. "This storm can wrench cars from the ground and wreck homes. I tell people when to find a safe place from the storm."she said.

Miss Wright asked, "Do you have questions for me?" The children put up their hands.

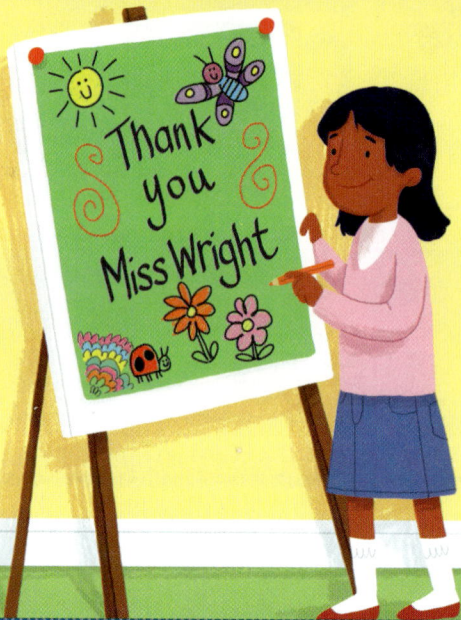

Josh asked, "Which month has the most big storms?"

"In our state, most storms happen in the winter," Miss Wright replied.

After Miss Wright left, the class wrote her a note. It said, "Thank you for teaching us about storms!"

A Lighthouse Stops Wrecks

In the past, ships counted on a lighthouse to stay safe. A light showed the way in bad storms or in fog. Ships and crews were safe.

A lighthouse keeper worked all year round. Month after month, he flicked his wrist to flip on the light. The light sent out beams at night.

The lighthouse lit up safe places for ships to sail. If a ship made a wrong turn, it could be wrecked on the rocks.

Ann Taylor-Hughes/iStockphoto/Getty Images

The lighthouse keeper had many jobs. There was no question that the keeper would help a ship.

The keeper also wrote notes in a log to keep track of storms. He tracked the wrecks. He could launch a rescue boat to help in a huge storm.

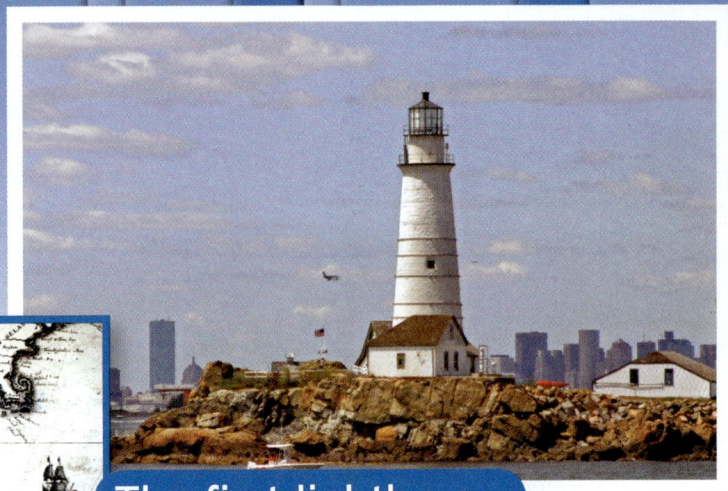

The first lighthouse in the U.S.

Lighthouse keepers have not been used for many years. There is just one lighthouse left in the U.S. with a keeper.

Now ships use other tools to stay safe. A lighthouse reminds us of the past. It is still a nice place for grown-ups and children to visit.

Jeremy D'Entremont, www.lighthouse.cc/Moment Open/Getty Images, (inset) manuel velasco/E+/Getty Images

Know About Snowstorms

Winter can be a fun time of the year. In some places, a winter month means the chance of a snowstorm. Children can play in the snow.

65

Listen to the news.

Do you know what to do in case of a big snowstorm? If you have been tuned to the news, you will know the storm is on the way. Stock up on food and water. Also fix up a first-aid kit. Grown-ups should fill up their cars with gas. Ask the right questions and check on good friends.

maxximmm/iStockphoto/Getty Images; (r)Jack Hollel/McGraw-Hill Education

The snowstorm hits! The snowflakes may fall as big as pennies or as small as gnats. The snow can pile up fast. This is the time to stay inside!

The wind can blow the snow into drifts. These drifts can be knee-deep or higher! Stay inside while the snowstorm is still blowing.

Glow Images

Dress right to go outside. Get
a warm coat, knit hat, mittens
and boots. Outside, the raw wind
can make you gnash those teeth.
Knowing what to do in the snow
is a good plan.

Don't forget to have fun in the
snow, too!

The Rusty Knight

One day a knight named Norm
saw a fine garden. He saw a
bench made of gnarled wood.
Norm decided to take a short nap.

While Norm slept, it rained. Norm's suit got rusty, but he didn't know it. When he awoke, Norm didn't know how long he had been asleep. Was it a day, a month, or a whole year?

A gnat buzzed around Norm's head. He tried to brush it away, but he could not move his arm.

Norm tried to sit up. He could not kneel or stand. Norm was rusted!

"I am stuck!" yelped Norm. "Help!"

A group of garden gnomes came by. These gnomes had a knack for being helpful. The head gnome gnawed his lip. Then, the gnome made a plan.

One gnome got a sharp knife. He cut up sandpaper. Each gnome took a piece of it. Then, they rubbed away all the rust on Norm's suit. Their work paid off.

Norm said, "Thank you! That rainy nap has taught me to always sleep in a dry place from now on!"

Three Shrimp

The king sat down on his throne. He clapped his hands. "Striped fish for supper, please!" he screeched. He gave the same order each night.

The cook heard the king's order.
He scratched his head. He did not
know what to do. Today there
were no striped fish from the
stream. The cook only had three
plump shrimp. The cook had to
think fast. He split each shrimp in
two and put them on a plate. He
spread the sauce on top.

The meal was set before the king. The king took a bite. He threw down his fork and gave his plate a push.

"This fish tastes strange," said the king. "It is not my order!"

The cook stood in front of the king. "Sir, I had no striped fish."

The king gnawed on a bit more shrimp. Then, the king shrugged.

The king smiled, "I think I like your shrimp better than the striped fish! Tomorrow I will eat shrimp again."

Each night the king had three shrimp with sauce on top!

A Thrilling Dance

You will not see a dragon before your eyes in real life. But you may see one at Chinese New Year. You may even see a dragon dance!

People think the dragon is a sign of good luck. The dragon costume is made with bamboo strips woven together to make a frame for the dragon.

Then fabric is made from red thread. Scales are drawn on the fabric. The fabric is wrapped on the frame.

The splendid costume is ready. It is time for the dragon dance. A trained team holds the dragon up on poles. A man stands out in front with a ball on a stick. He will lead the dance. He moves the ball all around. The dragon will follow the ball. Drums can be heard on the street.

The people holding the dragon stride down the street. They push the poles up and down. The dragon's nose almost scrapes the street!

More people strike drums and blow shrill horns. It is a fun, noisy party. What a thrilling way to ring in the Chinese New Year!

A Pair at the Fair

It was early July when the town threw a fair. A pair of young mice began to wonder why so many mice had gone to the fair.

The pair could see many kinds of stands. One mouse said, "Look! It's a dairy stand! Let's get a favorite food. Cheese! Just a scrap or shred is enough."

The other mouse said, "We can also drink milk through a straw! I will try to find a chair and sit. "

The mice found stairs and went up to drink some milk. Just then a loud noise gave them a big surprise. The mice fell in the milk with a splash! Their hair got all wet and white. What a mess! The mice got out of the milk and sprinted away.

Then, they looked and saw a few mice screaming on a fun ride. Soon they took a turn of their own.

As the mice left the fair that night, they saw a huge flag in the air. It was red, white and blue. It had stars and stripes. Then, the pair knew why all the mice were there.

Lights in the Air

When people get together for a holiday, they enjoy many things. They have fairs. They eat lots of food. People can also light up the air!

85

Do you wonder what might light up the air? Fireworks! Lights seem to splash across the sky in big shapes. These bright lights make a strong noise. The noise is loud enough to make young children scream! Watch the lights and your hair may even stand up!

You might see fireworks in July, on New Year's Eve, or a few other days. You may see them outside or upstairs from your window. They are fairly easy to see because they spread across the night sky. You need to watch closely because the lights shrink away and then are gone.

87

In July, watch the night sky. You might see big fireworks light up. They may come one at a time, in pairs, or in a big group. The lights look like pictures in the night sky. For many of us, seeing these lights are the best. It's a favorite thrill in the air!

by toonman/Moment/Getty Images

The Bears Prepare a Feast

It was late in fall, and the bears were aware that it was time to give thanks. The bears declared that it was their favorite time of year.

The bears still had a few days to prepare. Mama Bear and Papa Bear went to find food. They made the two young bears swear that they would help, too.

While Mama and Papa were gone, the young bears looked for food by their home. They found three pears and split each pear in two.

Mama and Papa came home
with a few shrimp and some corn.
They also got a surprise for the
young bears. It was a big fish!

Mama said, "Go scrub your paws
and wear your best shirts. Papa
and I will prepare the food with
care. Then, we will sit and share!"

The bears sat down for their feast. The bears felt so grateful. The young bears stared at the food with wonder. They wanted to eat it all up!

Papa said, "First, let's say thanks. Then, we can share this feast!"

Leaders Care

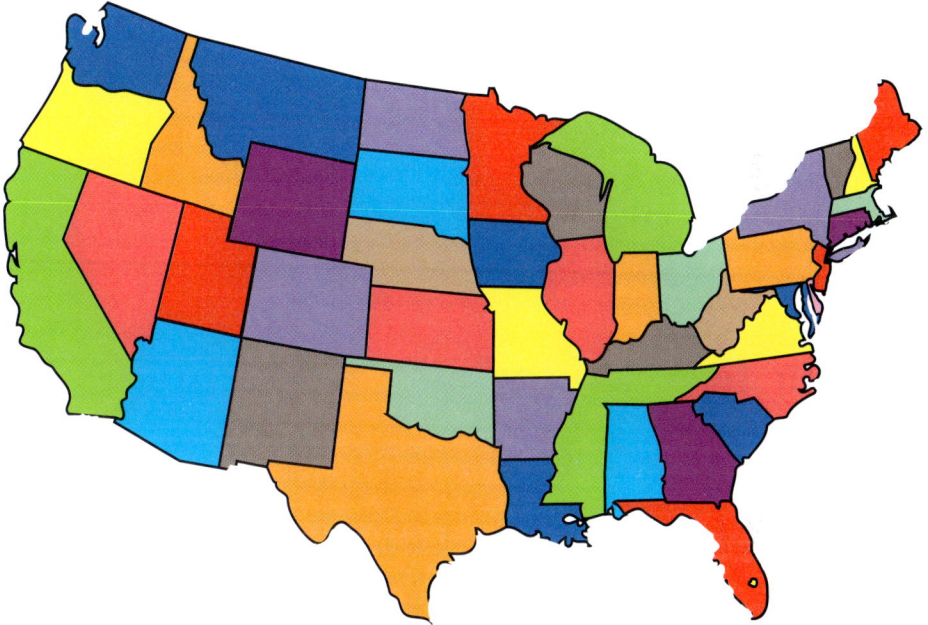

In winter, we declare how much we care for the people who lead the nation. Some of these men are gone, but we know they did well!

93

Our first leader was this man. Do you wonder what his life was like? He was a strong leader who had to fight to be free. He may have been scared, but he cared enough to fight the threat that our new nation felt. He was brave and strong!

Do you know this man? When he was young, he shared a small log house. When he was older, he liked to wear a tall black hat. It was his favorite.

It was not a surprise when he declared that all people should be treated fairly. He felt that the laws should be the same for all.

Can you name other leaders? Are you aware how these people helped make rules and laws?

So, when you go to school, drive in a car, or say what is on your mind, think of these people. We are proud of our leaders!

DECODABLE WORDS

Target Phonics Elements
  Variant Vowel Spellings with
  Digraphs, *oo:* cool, goose, moon,
  rooster, roots, scooped, smoother,
  soon, zoo

HIGH-FREQUENCY WORDS

answer, brought, busy, door,
enough, eyes
Review: animal, are, come,
have, know, other, said, should,
they, through, to together,
was, you

Choose a Room   WORD COUNT: 175

DECODABLE WORDS

Target Phonics Elements
  Variant Vowel Spellings with
  Digraphs, *oo*: broom, choose, food,
  loose, noon, pool, roof, room, rooms,
  scoop, spoons, too, tools, zoo

HIGH-FREQUENCY WORDS

brought, busy, enough, eyes
Review: all, any, have, move,
other, some, to, together, you

The Flute Youth   WORD COUNT: 171

DECODABLE WORDS

Target Phonics Elements
  Variant Vowel Spellings with Digraphs,
  u_e, ou; u_e: dudes, flute, flutes, Jude,
  June, tunes; ***ou:*** cougars, coupon, group,
  you, youth

HIGH-FREQUENCY WORDS

answer, brought, busy, door,
enough, eyes
Review: are, buy, have, listen,
many, of, one, said, should,
they, to, what

Group Rules   WORD COUNT: 176

DECODABLE WORDS

Target Phonics Elements
  Variant Vowel Spellings with
  Digraphs, *u_e, ou; u_e:* rude, rule,
  rules; ***ou:*** group, soup, you, youth

HIGH-FREQUENCY WORDS

brought, busy, door, enough
Review: are, all, another, any,
are, could done, one, people,
should, sure, they, to, together

Lewis and His New Suit   WORD COUNT: 179

DECODABLE WORDS

Target Phonics Elements
  Variant Vowel Spellings with
  Digraphs, *ew, ui; ew:* blew, crew, drew,
  Lewis, new; ***ui:*** fruit, fruity, juice, suit,
  suitcase

HIGH-FREQUENCY WORDS

answer, brought, busy, door,
enough, eyes
Review: any, from, have, one,
soon, there, they, to, was, what,
who

97

A Cruise Crew

DECODABLE WORDS
Target Phonics Elements
Variant Vowel Spellings with Digraphs, *ew, ui; ew:* blew, chew crew, new; ***ui:*** bruise, cruise, fruit, juice, suits

HIGH-FREQUENCY WORDS
answer, brought, busy, door, enough
Review: all, because, been, call, have, of, out, people, some, sure, there, they, to, together, you

Sue and Lucy

DECODABLE WORDS
Target Phonics Elements
Variant Vowel Spellings with Digraphs, *ue, u; ue:* blue, bluebird, glue, Sue, true; ***u:*** flu, Lucy, students, super, truth

HIGH-FREQUENCY WORDS
answer, brought, busy, door, enough, eyes
Review: all, are, could, do, from, of, one, said, school, to, together, they, was, you

A True Team

DECODABLE WORDS
Target Phonics Elements
Variant Vowel Spellings with Digraphs, *ue, u; ue:* bluebird, clues, cruel, glue, true, untrue; ***u:*** Pluto, students, super, truth

HIGH-FREQUENCY WORDS
answer, busy, door, enough, eyes
Review: another, do, done, have, of, one, other, should, they, to, together, too, want, would

Week 2 ### Paul's Paw

DECODABLE WORDS
Target Phonics Elements
Variant Vowel Spellings with Digraphs *au, aw; au:* because, fault, haul, Paul, pause; ***aw:*** awful, bawl, crawl, jaw, paw, saw

HIGH-FREQUENCY WORDS
brother, father, friend, love, mother, picture
Review: call, come, does, have, of, once, said, some, they, to, was, would

Thank You Authors!

DECODABLE WORDS
Target Phonics Elements
Variant Vowel Spellings with Digraphs *au, aw; au:* author, authors, autos, cause, haunted, launch, pause; ***aw:*** dawn, draw, hawk, lawn, yawn

HIGH-FREQUENCY WORDS
brother, father, friend, love, mother, picture
Review: all, call, into, of, some, they, to, together, what, who, would

Not Too Small

DECODABLE WORDS

Target Phonics Elements
  Variant Vowel Spellings with
  Digraphs *a, augh; a:* all, also,
  always, ball, fall, small, smaller;
  augh: caught, taught

HIGH-FREQUENCY WORDS

brother, father, friend, love,
mother, picture
Review: answered, every, good,
over, they, to, together, too,
very, want, was

My Baseball Coach

DECODABLE WORDS

Target Phonics Elements
  Variant Vowel Spellings with
  Digraphs *a, augh; a:* always, ball,
  fall, baseball, called, small; *augh:*
  caught, daughter, daughters,
  naughty, taught

HIGH-FREQUENCY WORDS

brother, father, friend, love,
mother, picture
Review: another, any, comes,
from, of, oh, one, to, was

A Walk With Mayor Moose

DECODABLE WORDS

Target Phonics Elements
  Variant Vowel Spellings with Digraph
  al: chalk, stalks, talk, talks, talked, walk,
  walks, walked

HIGH-FREQUENCY WORDS

brother, father, friend, love,
mother, picture
Review: again, another, any,
are, could, do, of, said, they,
through, to, who

Teacher Talk

DECODABLE WORDS

Target Phonics Elements
  Variant Vowel Spellings with Digraph
  al: chalk, stalk, talk, talks, talked, walk,
  walked

HIGH-FREQUENCY WORDS

brother, father, friend, love,
mother
Review: also, answer, do, great,
know, other, learned, people,
school, some, they, to, want,
would

DECODABLE WORDS
Target Phonics Elements
  Silent Letters *wr:* wreck, wrench, Wright, wrong, wrote

HIGH-FREQUENCY WORDS
been, children, question, month, their, year
Review: are, do, great, from, have, of, people, picture, said, there, to, was

A Lighthouse Stops Wrecks

WORD COUNT: 175

DECODABLE WORDS
Target Phonics Elements
  Silent Letters *wr:* wrecked, wrecks, wrist, wrong, wrote

HIGH-FREQUENCY WORDS
been, children, question, month, year
Review: could, have, many, of, one, other, there, to, was, would

Know About Snowstorms

WORD COUNT: 187

DECODABLE WORDS
Target Phonics Elements
  Silent Letters *gn, kn; gn:* gnash, gnats; *kn:* knit, knock, know, knowing

HIGH-FREQUENCY WORDS
been, children, question, month, year
Review: any, are, do, have, into, of, should, some, sure, they, to, warm, water, what

The Rusty Knight

WORD COUNT: 188

DECODABLE WORDS
Target Phonics Elements
  Silent Letters *gn, kn; gn:* gnarled, gnat, gnawed, gnome, gnomes; *kn:* knack, kneel, knew, knife, knight, know

HIGH-FREQUENCY WORDS
been, month, their, year
Review: could, move, of, one, only, said, to, was

Three Shrimp

DECODABLE WORDS

Target Phonics Elements
  Three-letter Blends, *scr, spl,*
  spr, str, thr, shr; scr: scratched,
  screeched; ***spl:*** split; ***spr:*** spread; ***str:***
  strange, stream, striped; ***thr:*** three,
  threw, throne; ***shr:*** shrimp, shrugged

HIGH-FREQUENCY WORDS

before, heard, front, push,
tomorrow, your
Review: again, do, from, of,
only, said, there, to, today, two,
was, what

A Thrllling Dance

DECODABLE WORDS

Target Phonics Elements
  Three-letter Blends, *scr, spl,*
  spr, str, thr, shr; scr: scrapes; ***spl:***
  splendid; ***spr:*** spread; ***str:*** street,
  stride, strike, strips; ***thr:*** thread,
  thrilling; ***shr:*** shrill

HIGH-FREQUENCY WORDS

before, heard, front, push, your
Review: are, eyes, from, moves,
of, one, people, they, to,
together, what, year

A Pair at the Fair

DECODABLE WORDS

Target Phonics Elements
  r*-controlled Vowels, *air: air, chair, dairy,
  fair, hair, pair, stairs

HIGH-FREQUENCY WORDS

favorite, few, gone, surprise,
wonder, young
Review: could, do, early,
enough, many, of, one, other,
said, some, their, there, they,
through, to, was, what

Lights in the Air

DECODABLE WORDS

Target Phonics Elements
  r*-controlled Vowels, *air: air, fairs,
  fairly, hair, pairs, upstairs

HIGH-FREQUENCY WORDS

favorite, few, gone, wonder,
young
Review: are, because, children,
come, do, enough, from, have,
many, of, one, other, people,
pictures, they, to, together,
what, year's, your

The Bears Prepare a Feast

DECODABLE WORDS
Target Phonics Elements
r-controlled Vowels, *are, ear; are:*
aware, care, declared, prepare,
share, stared; *ear:* bear, bears, pear,
pears, swear, wear

HIGH-FREQUENCY WORDS
favorite, few, gone, surprise,
wonder, young
Review: give, of, said, some,
their, they, to, two, was, would,
your

Leaders Care

DECODABLE WORDS
Target Phonics Elements
r-controlled Vowels, *are, ear; are:*
aware, care, declare, scared, share;
ear: wear

HIGH-FREQUENCY WORDS
favorite, few, gone, surprise,
wonder, young
Review: another, are, been,
do, enough, have, of, others,
people, school, some, they, to,
was, what, who

HIGH-FREQUENCY WORDS TAUGHT TO DATE

Kindergarten

a
and
are
can
come
do
does
for
go
good
has
have
help
here
I
is
like
little
look
me
my
of
play
said
see
she
the
they
this
to
too
want
was
we
what
where

Grade I

who
with
you

about
above
after
again
ago
all
animal
another
answer
any
around
away
be
been
before
began
better
blue
boy
brother
brought
build
busy
buy
by
call
carry
caught
children
climb
color

come
could
day
does
done
door
down
early
eat
eight
enough
every
eyes
fall
father
favorite
few
find
flew
food
found
four
friend
from
front
full
fun
girl
give
gone
good
great
green
grow
guess
happy

hard
heard
help
her
how
instead
into
jump
knew
know
large
laugh
learn
listen
live
love
make
many
money
month
more
mother
move
near
new
no
none
not
nothing
now
of
oh
old
once
one
only

or
other
our
out
over
people
picture
place
poor
pretty
pull
push
put
question
right
round
run
school
should
small
so
some
soon
start
sure
surprise
their
then
there
they
thought
three
through
today
together
tomorrow

too
toward
two
under
up
upon
very
use
walk
want
warm
water
way
were
what
who
why
woman
wonder
work
would
write
year
young
your

DECODING SKILLS TAUGHT TO DATE

Short *a*; -s inflection endings; Short *i*; double final consonants; beginning consonant blends: *bl* blends, *cl* blends, *fl* blends, *gl* blends, *pl* blends, *sl* blends; -s (plural nouns); short *o*; alphabetical order (one letter); beginning consonant blends: *r*-blends; *s*-blends; possessives; short *e* spelled *e* and *ea*; inflection ending -ed (no spelling change); short *u*; contractions with '*s*; ending consonant blends *nd, nk, st, sk, mp*; inflection ending *ing* (no spelling change); consonant digraphs *th, sh, ng*; closed syllables; digraphs *ch, wh, ph* and trigraph -*tch*; -es (plural nouns); long *a, a_e*; contractions with *not*; long *i, i_e*; plurals (with CVCe syllables); soft *c*; soft *g, dge*; -*ing* (drop the final *e*); long *o, o_e*; long *u, u_e*; long *e, e_e*; CVCe syllables; variant vowel spellings with digraphs: *oo, u*; inflection endings -ed and -ing (double final consonant); long *a*: *a, ai, ay*; alphabetical order (two letters); long *e*: *e, ee, ea, ie*; prefixes *re-, un-, pre-*; long *o*: *o, oa, ow, oe*; open syllables; long *i*: *i, y, igh, ie*; inflectional endings; long *e*: *y, ey*; compound words; r-controlled vowel *ar*; plurals (irregular); r-controlled vowels *er, ir, ur, or*; r-controlled vowels *or, ore, oar*; dipthongs *ou, ow*; comparative inflectional endings -*er*, -*est*; dipthongs *oy, oi*; final stable syllables; variant vowel spellings with digraphs: *oo, u, u_e, ew, ue, ui, ou*; suffixes -*ful* and -*less*; variant vowel spellings with digraphs: *a, aw, au, augh, al*; vowel-team syllables; silent letters *wr, kn, gn*; compound words; three-letter blends *scr, spl, spr, str, thr, shr*; inflectional endings -*ed*, -*ing*; r-controlled vowels *air, are, ear*; r-controlled vowel syllables